EASY WAYS TO MAKE MONEY ONLINE

EVEN WITH YOUR SMARTPHONE

Dedication

This book is dedicated to God Almighty and my family, the Mokobia family.

CONTENTS

Introduction

- Any form of business transaction that occurs through the internet is considered an Online Business. Trading online or offering an online services are examples of online businesses. This is a form of business that mainly operate via the internet. Most of these are used for side hustles in order to meet up with some demands.
- Working online is also something one can do in the comfort of his home, at his leisure and whenever he decides to. But mind you, perseverance and consistency are two keys to a successful business as the way to success is not all smooth.
- Welcome and benefit from this knowledge…

Freelancing?

Freelancing is a contract-based profession where instead of being recruited in an , the person uses his skills and experience to provide services to a number of clients.

In simple terms, freelancing is when you use your skills,

education, and experience to work with multiple clients and take on various assignments without committing to a single employer. The number of assignments or tasks that you can take just boils down to your ability to deliver on them as asked from them.

Freelancing usually involves jobs (called gigs) that allow you to work-from-home situations. But don't associate freelancing as the same as having a work-from-home job.

Freelancing is an enticing profession. It takes care of almost all the problems of a usual service-class human. Freelancers work an average of 11 hours less per week than full-time employed workers.

That adds up to about 550 hours per year or 23 whole days.

- **How To Become A Freelancer?**

Becoming a freelancer is just as easy as ordering something over the Internet. You visit sites that offer freelance jobs and tasks and take them on. This is a wonderful way of starting out and getting your name out there.

Here are a few sites that you can try for freelancing jobs:

- **What Is Freelancing?**
- **How To Become A Freelancer?**

The phrase 'I am a freelancer' gets thrown about a lot nowadays when someone is asked about what he does for a living. It could be a friend, colleague, or even your family member who left his regular 9 to 5 job to become a freelancer.

Many reasons contribute to this sudden shift in the mentality of people's perception about jobs per se causing them to shift to freelancing.

But why do they do that?

Can freelancers sustain for long without a job?

What exactly do these "freelancers" do?

And how do freelancers make money?

Here's a comprehensive guide to answer all your questions.

- **What Is Freelancing?**

Freelancing is a contract-based profession where instead of being recruited in an organisation, the person uses his skills and experience to provide services to a number of clients.

In simple terms, freelancing is when you use your skills, education, and experience to work with multiple clients and take on various assignments without committing to a single employer. The number of assignments or tasks that you can take just boils down to your ability to deliver on them as asked from them.

Freelancing usually involves jobs (called gigs) that allow you to work-from-home situations. But don't associate freelancing as the same as having a work-from-home job.

Freelancing doesn't always mean that you'll work from home. You might have to work at your client's office too depending upon the type of work and the client's requirements.

A work from home job involves a contract between you and a single employer who gives you a salary while freelancing doesn't.

It is just that many of the jobs that freelancers perform can be delivered over the Internet without their presence at the company or clients place.

• Who Is A Freelancer?

A freelancer or freelance worker is a self-employed person who earns money by providing services to multiple clients. These services relate to the person's skills and are not necessarily provided to just businesses.

Freelancers either use third-party platforms like Fiverr, 99designs, etc. to get business or use their network to get more business and provide services to their clients directly.

But is it a good choice for a career? Can you sustain a lavish life while freelancing? How do you start with freelancing jobs?

Well, when 11 percent of the working adult population in the United States is working primarily as full-time freelancers, there must be something good about this industry.

Freelancing As A Career

The rise of freelancers has resulted in the development of a new concept – the gig economy. In the gig economy, a person, instead of working for a single employer full-time and getting a fixed salary in return, works for multiple clients at his own terms and at a price he thinks his work deserves.

Freelancing is an enticing profession. It takes care of almost all the problems of a usual service-class human. According to Upwork, Americans work an average of 47 hours per week. Freelancers work an average of 11 hours less per week than full-time employed workers. That adds up to about 550 hours per year or 23 whole days.

Full-time traditional workers spend nearly an additional full month each year behind the keyboard (or wherever they work).

All this along with advantages like freedom to work from anywhere at a time of your choice, being your own boss, keeping all the profits, and a lower cost of operating surely attracts a lot of people to take freelancing as careers.

•How to become a freelancer?

Becoming a freelancer is just as easy as ordering something over the Internet. You visit sites that offer freelance jobs and tasks and take them on. This is a wonderful way of starting out and getting your name out there.

Here are a few sites that you can try for freelancing jobs:

- **Fiverr:** The world's largest marketplace to look for freelance jobs. Just create an account post what you can do, add few links and you're done.

- **99Designs:** A perfect place to find freelancing jobs if you're a designer.

- **Upwork:** Upwork is a more professional looking freelance marketplace where you'll find more business clients.

- **Freelancer.com:** Freelancer.com is among the oldest freelance job marketplace which you can choose in your initial year when you have little or no freelance experience.

AFFILIATE MARKETING

- **A**ffiliate marketing is the process by which an affiliate earns a commission for marketing another person's or company's products. The affiliate simply searches for a product they enjoy, then promotes that product and earns a piece of the profit from each sale they make.

The sales are tracked via affiliate links from one website to another.

Affiliate marketing is a great way to drive sales and generate significant online revenue. Extremely beneficial to both brands and affiliate marketers, the new push toward less traditional marketing tactics has certainly paid off.

•How Do Affiliate Marketers Get Paid?

A quick and inexpensive method of making money without the hassle of actually selling a product, affiliate marketing has an undeniable draw for those looking to increase their income online. But how does an affiliate get paid after linking the seller to the consumer?

- **Pay per sale.**

This is the standard affiliate marketing structure. In this program, the merchant pays the affiliate a percentage of the sale price of the product after the consumer purchases the product as a result of affiliate marketing strategies. In other words, the affiliate must actually get the investor to invest in the affiliate product before they are compensated.

- **Pay per click.**
Affiliate marketing is largely about generating traffic to websites and trying to get customers to click and take action. So, the myth that affiliate marketing is all about SEO (search engine optimization) is no surprise.

Ecommerce

Affiliate Marketing

What it is and How to Get

Started

Affiliate Marketing Social

Generic

Create Your Own Store and

Start Selling Today

START YOUR FREE TRIAL

What if you could make money at any time, from anywhere — even while you sleep?

This is the concept behind affiliate marketing.

Affiliate marketing is the process by which an affiliate earns a commission for marketing another person's or company's products. The affiliate simply searches for a product they enjoy, then promotes that product and earns a piece of the profit from each sale they make. The sales are tracked via affiliate links from one website to another.

- **Article Image Affiliate Marketing Social BigCommerce**

Affiliate marketing is a great way to drive sales and generate significant online revenue. Extremely beneficial to both brands and affiliate marketers, the new push toward less traditional marketing tactics has certainly paid off.

In fact, affiliate marketing spend in the United States increased from $5.4 billion in 2017 to $8.2 billion in 2022 — which means there's plenty of room for those looking to get a piece of the pie.

This step-by-step beginner's guide will walk you through

how to launch your affiliating marketing business and what benefits you can expect.

- **How Does Affiliate Marketing Work?**

Because affiliate marketing works by spreading the responsibilities of product marketing and creation across parties, it leverages the abilities of a variety of individuals for a more effective marketing strategy while providing contributors with a share of the profit. To make this work, three different parties must be involved:

Seller and product creators.
The affiliate or advertiser.
The consumer.

Let's delve into the complex relationship these three parties share to ensure affiliate marketing is a success:

Seller and product creators. The seller, whether a solo entrepreneur or large enterprise, is a vendor, merchant, product creator or retailer with a product to market. The product can be a physical object, like household goods, or a service, like makeup tutorials.

Also known as the brand, the seller does not need to be actively involved in the marketing, but they may also be the advertiser and profit from the revenue sharing associated with affiliate marketing.

For example, the seller could be an ecommerce merchant that started a dropshipping business and wants to reach a new audience by paying affiliate sites to promote their products. Or the seller could be a SaaS company that leverages affiliates to help sell their marketing software.

The affiliate or publisher. Also known as a publisher, the affiliate can be either an individual or a company that markets the seller's product in an appealing way to potential consumers. In other words, the affiliate promotes the product to persuade consumers that it is valuable or beneficial to them and convince them to purchase the product. If the consumer does end up buying the product, the affiliate receives a portion of the revenue made.

Affiliates often have a very specific audience to whom they market, generally adhering to that audience's interests. This creates a defined niche or personal brand that helps the affiliate attract consumers who will be most likely to act on the promotion.

The consumer.
Of course, for the affiliate system to work, there needs to be sales — and the

consumer or customer is the one who makes them happen.

The affiliate will market the product/service to consumers through the necessary channel(s), whether it be social media, a blog or a YouTube video, and if the consumer deems the product as valuable or beneficial to them, then they can follow the affiliate link and checkout on the merchant's website. If the customer does purchase the item, then the affiliate receives a portion of the revenue made.

However, keep in mind that the customer must be aware that you, the affiliate, are receiving a commission off the product.

According to the Federal Trade Commission, an affiliate marketer must clearly and conspicuously disclose their relationship to the retailer, thus allowing the consumer to decide how much weight to give your endorsement.

A disclaimer such as "The products I'm going to use in this video were given to me by Company X" gives your viewers the information they need and allows them to make an informed decision about whether or not to buy the affiliate product.

Types of Affiliate Marketing

It's often unclear whether an affiliate marketer has actually used the product they're promoting or if they're simply in it for the money — sometimes it may not matter to the customer one way or the other.

But other times, such as with diet services or skincare products, the customer may not trust an affiliate unless they know that he/she has tested and approved the product themselves.

In 2009, renowned affiliate marketer Pat Flynn categorized affiliate marketing into three types — unattached, related and involved — to help differentiate between affiliate marketers who are closely tied to a product versus those who are not.

Here we'll break down each category to help you decide which route to take.

Unattached.
In the unattached business model, the affiliate marketer has no connection to the

product or service they are promoting. They have no expertise or authority in the niche of the product, nor can they make claims about its use.

Typically, an unattached affiliate will run PPC (pay-per-click) marketing campaigns, using an affiliate link in hopes that shoppers will click it and make a purchase on their own.

While unattached affiliate marketing may be attractive due to its lack of commitment, it's generally for those who simply want to generate an income without investing in the product or customer relationship.

Related.

A happy medium between unattached and involved, related affiliate marketing is for those who don't necessarily use the product or service, but who are somehow related to the niche audience. These affiliates often have some sort of influence in the niche and an established following, and can therefore offer some authority.

For example, perhaps you're promoting a clothing brand you've never used before, but you have an audience through a fashion blog or YouTube channel. In this case, you would be considered a related affiliate marketer.

The advantage of this type of affiliate marketing is that the affiliate has the expertise to generate traffic, however they may risk recommending a bad product or service if they've never actually used it before, potentially costing them the trust of their audience.

Involved.

As the name suggests, involved affiliate marketing describes those who are closely tied to the product or service they're promoting. The affiliate has tried the product themselves, trusts that it will provide a good experience and has the authority to make claims about its use.

Rather than relying on pays per click, involved affiliate marketers use their personal experiences with the product in their marketing efforts, and customers can trust them as reliable sources of information.

Of course, this type of affiliate marketing requires more legwork and time to build credibility, but it will likely result in greater payoffs down the road.

- **How Do Affiliate Marketers Get Paid?**

A quick and inexpensive method of making money without the hassle of actually selling a product, affiliate marketing has an undeniable draw for those looking to increase their income online. But how does an affiliate get paid after linking the seller to the consumer?

The answer can get complicated.

The consumer doesn't always need to buy the product for the affiliate to get a kickback. Depending on the program, the affiliate's contribution to the seller's sales will be measured differently.

The affiliate may get paid in various ways:

- **Pay per sale.** This is the standard affiliate marketing structure. In this program, the merchant pays the affiliate a percentage of the sale price of the product after the consumer purchases the product as a result of affiliate marketing strategies. In other words, the affiliate must actually get the investor to invest in the affiliate product before they are compensated.

- **Pay per lead.**

A more complex system, pay per lead affiliate marketing programs compensates the affiliate based on the conversion of leads. The affiliate must persuade the consumer to visit the merchant's website and complete the desired action — whether it's filling out a contact form, signing up for a trial of a product, subscribing to a newsletter or downloading software or files.

- **Pay per click.** Affiliate marketing is largely about generating traffic to websites and trying to get customers to click and take action. So, the myth that affiliate marketing is all about SEO (search engine optimization) is no surprise.

However, while organic traffic is free, SEO simply can't sustain affiliate marketers in such a saturated market — which is why some affiliate marketers utilize PPC.

- **PPC (pay per click)** programs focus on the affiliate to redirect consumers from their marketing platform to the merchant's website. This means the affiliate must engage the consumer to the extent that they will move from the affiliate's site to the merchant's site. The affiliate is paid based on the increase in web traffic.

There are two common concepts in PPC:

CPA (cost-per-acquisition): With this model, the affiliate gets paid each time the seller or retailer acquires a lead, which is when an affiliate link takes the customer to the merchant's online store and they take an action, such as subscribing to an email list or filling out a "Contact Us" form.

EPC (earnings-per-click): This is the measure for the average earnings per 100 clicks for all affiliates in a retailer's affiliate program.

Pay per install.

In this payout system, the affiliate gets paid each time they direct a user to the merchant's website and installs a product, generally a mobile app or software.

So, if a retailer budgets for a $0.10 bid for each install generated via an affiliate program, and the campaign results in 1,000 installs, then the retailer will pay ($0.10 x 1,000) = $100.

- ## Why Be an Affiliate Marketer?

- ## Passive income.

While any "regular" job requires you to be at work to make money, affiliate marketing offers you the ability to make money while you sleep. By investing an initial amount of time into a campaign, you will see continuous returns on that time as consumers purchase the product over the following days and weeks. You receive money for your work long after you've finished it. Even when you're not in front of your computer, your marketing skills will be earning you a steady flow of income.

• Complete Online Surveys

It might sound too good to be true, but you can earn extra cash by completing surveys online.

Many companies pay people to participate in surveys for general market research and consumer behavior analysis. These surveys help companies make business decisions, like what types of products to launch or where to publish advertisements.

- **Swagbucks.** Watch videos, play games, and complete online surveys to earn points. Then, redeem them for cash or gift cards.

- **Survey Junkie.** Help brands deliver better products and services by participating in their market surveys.

- **Harris Poll Online**. Enter a rewards program by answering polls run by this survey platform.

BLOGGING

You can start a blog about any topic. Researching popular blog ideas can help you find a profitable niche. Some blog niche examples include travel blogs, food blogs, and book blogs.

The most common ways to make money blogging are through advertising, affiliate marketing, brand sponsorships, and selling products.

Tutor Students Online

If selling digital courses isn't your thing, but you're still interested in teaching, consider becoming an online tutor.

Many students today actively look for remote lessons. Independent tutors often offer their services via video communication apps like Zoom and Skype and accept payments via PayPal.

Make money by giving on-demand lessons and providing personalized feedback. You will create lesson plans, learning modules, and keep track of the student's progress.

Make sure to evaluate your expertise when choosing a topic to teach. Popular tutoring subjects include math, languages, and computer science.

Consider obtaining certification to enhance your credibility as an online tutor and improve rates. And before giving live lessons, set up a strong internet connection to ensure smooth video communication.

When ready, create a website or join an online tutoring platform to promote your services. Here are four popular platforms for people interested in the online tutoring business:

- **Skooli.** Schedule lessons in advance or accept them whenever you're online.

- **TutorMe.com**: Connects students with tutors based on their needs and preferences.

- **Tutor.com.** Offers tutors based in the United States the opportunity to teach 250+ subjects to students of varying ages and education levels.

- **Preply.com:** Teach different languages and set custom rates for your services

Become a Graphic Designer

An average base salary of around **$58,000/year** makes graphic design another high-paying career worth pursuing. For creative individuals, it's an excellent way of making money online.

The career path of a graphic designer is similar to a web developer. After choosing a specialization, the next step is to learn the required skills. Many design courses are available on various eLearning platforms to help you get started.

For example, a web designer must study user experience, user interface, and the basics of HTML and CSS. Meanwhile, a logo designer should master color theory, typography, and design tools like **Adobe Illustrator** and **CorelDRAW.**

Here are some of the best sites to make money online via graphic design gigs:

- **DesignCrowd.** Offers a wide range of projects, from logo and website to billboard design.
- **Minty.** Ideal for skilled artists looking for design projects with automatically generated contracts.
- **We Work Remotely.** Find different types of remote design jobs.

- **99designs.** Provides high-quality graphic design services in numerous categories, such as websites and apps, clothing and merchandise, as well as business and advertising.

BECOME AN INFLUENCER

The continuous rise of social media has made influencer marketing a popular choice to make money online.

Like affiliate marketing, companies pay influencers with large followings to market their products and services. The main difference is influencers aim to impact people's buying decisions instead of simply bringing leads. Like streamers, how much money influencers make significantly depends on their following.

The most critical aspects of being a profitable influencer are cultivating a personal brand and becoming an .authoritative voice within your niche. This will help attract sponsors and advertisers.

Although many influencers are on Instagram, you can take advantage of other platforms like YouTube and Twitter to build a following and create

different types of content. Learn which content types work best for each platform. The social media platform TikTok, for example, is excellent for people who want to create viral videos.

Offer Digital Marketing Services

Help business owners attract their target audiences and improve sales performance by offering marketing services. These services may include SEO strategies and social media management.

It's a great way to make money if you're already familiar with these concepts or want to develop your skills further.

SEO services can help sites rank higher on search engine results pages (SERP), receive more traffic, and generate leads. You must have SEO skills like link building and keyword research to offer these services. On the other hand, providing social media management services means planning and executing marketing plans on various social platforms. These activities encourage better audience interaction and higher brand recognition.

When you're ready to monetize your skills, offer your services on job marketplaces like **Fiverr** and **Freelancer**. Consider applying to a marketing agency as a digital marketer for a long-term career in this field.

Summary

Don't ever feel like it's difficult, always try first. There's always a first time for something great. Not everyone is you and remember if you are broke, you are alone. Start now!...